50 Made From Scratch with Love Recipes for Home

By: Kelly Johnson

Table of Contents

- Fresh Homemade Pizza Dough
- Classic Beef Meatballs
- Creamy Macaroni and Cheese
- Soft and Fluffy Cinnamon Rolls
- Roasted Garlic Mashed Potatoes
- Perfect Chocolate Chip Cookies
- Homemade Spaghetti Sauce
- Fresh Lemonade from Scratch
- Homemade Vanilla Pudding
- Crispy Chicken Tenders
- Fresh Vegetable Soup
- Warm Buttermilk Biscuits
- Creamy Alfredo Sauce
- Sourdough Bread
- Homemade Bagels
- Classic Beef Stew
- Apple Pie with Homemade Crust

- Baked Ziti with Meatballs
- Creamy Tomato Soup
- Chicken Pot Pie
- Fresh Raspberry Jam
- Banana Bread from Scratch
- French Toast with Homemade Syrup
- Pulled Pork Sandwiches
- Homemade Granola Bars
- Focaccia Bread with Rosemary
- Fresh Guacamole with Salsa
- Homemade Chicken Noodle Soup
- Homemade Ice Cream
- Fresh Tortillas
- Sweet Potato Fries
- Classic Meatloaf
- Eggplant Parmesan
- Lemon Meringue Pie
- Homemade Chocolate Cake
- Perfect Scrambled Eggs

- Beef and Vegetable Stir Fry
- Rustic Italian Focaccia
- Fresh Peach Cobbler
- Homemade Donuts
- Baked Chicken Parmesan
- Creamy Mushroom Risotto
- Spicy Tuna Poke Bowl
- Homemade Scones with Jam
- Hearty Breakfast Burritos
- Classic Lasagna
- Slow Cooker Chili
- Creamy Shrimp Scampi
- Blueberry Muffins
- Chocolate Fudge Brownies

Fresh Homemade Pizza Dough

- Ingredients:

    1. 2 1/4 tsp active dry yeast
    2. 1 1/2 cups warm water
    3. 3 1/2 cups all-purpose flour
    4. 1 tsp salt
    5. 1 tbsp olive oil
    6. 1 tsp sugar

- Instructions:

    1. Dissolve yeast and sugar in warm water, let it sit for 5 minutes until foamy.
    2. Combine flour and salt in a bowl. Add yeast mixture and olive oil, stir to combine.
    3. Knead dough on a floured surface for about 8 minutes until smooth.
    4. Let dough rise in an oiled bowl, covered, for 1 hour or until doubled.
    5. Roll out dough and top with your favorite ingredients.

Classic Beef Meatballs

- Ingredients:
    1. 1 lb ground beef
    2. 1/2 cup breadcrumbs
    3. 1/4 cup grated Parmesan
    4. 1/4 cup milk
    5. 1 egg
    6. 2 cloves garlic, minced
    7. 1 tbsp Italian seasoning
    8. Salt and pepper to taste
- Instructions:
    1. Preheat oven to 375°F (190°C).
    2. Mix all ingredients in a bowl until well combined.
    3. Roll into 1-inch meatballs and place on a baking sheet.
    4. Bake for 20-25 minutes or until browned and cooked through.
    5. Serve with marinara sauce and pasta.

Creamy Macaroni and Cheese

- Ingredients:

    1. 1 lb elbow macaroni
    2. 2 cups shredded sharp cheddar cheese
    3. 1/2 cup grated Parmesan cheese
    4. 2 cups milk
    5. 1/4 cup butter
    6. 2 tbsp flour
    7. Salt and pepper to taste

- Instructions:

    1. Cook macaroni according to package instructions, then drain.
    2. In a saucepan, melt butter over medium heat, then stir in flour to form a roux.
    3. Gradually add milk, whisking to prevent lumps, and cook until thickened.
    4. Stir in cheddar and Parmesan until melted and smooth.
    5. Toss with cooked macaroni and season with salt and pepper.

Soft and Fluffy Cinnamon Rolls

- Ingredients:
    1. 2 1/4 tsp active dry yeast
    2. 1 cup warm milk
    3. 1/2 cup sugar
    4. 1/4 cup melted butter
    5. 2 eggs
    6. 4 cups all-purpose flour
    7. 1 tsp salt
    8. 1/2 cup brown sugar
    9. 2 tbsp ground cinnamon

- Instructions:
    1. Combine warm milk, yeast, and sugar. Let sit for 5 minutes.
    2. Mix in melted butter, eggs, flour, and salt to form a dough.
    3. Knead for 6-8 minutes, then let rise for 1 hour.
    4. Roll out dough, spread with butter, brown sugar, and cinnamon, then roll up.
    5. Slice into rolls, place in a greased pan, and let rise for 30 minutes.
    6. Bake at 350°F (175°C) for 20-25 minutes.

Roasted Garlic Mashed Potatoes

- Ingredients:

    1. 2 lbs potatoes, peeled and cubed
    2. 1 head garlic
    3. 1/2 cup butter
    4. 1/2 cup milk
    5. Salt and pepper to taste

- Instructions:

    1. Preheat oven to 400°F (200°C).
    2. Cut the top off the garlic head, drizzle with olive oil, and roast in foil for 30 minutes.
    3. Boil potatoes in salted water until tender, about 15 minutes.
    4. Mash the potatoes with butter, milk, and roasted garlic.
    5. Season with salt and pepper, then serve.

Perfect Chocolate Chip Cookies

- Ingredients:
    1. 1 cup butter, softened
    2. 3/4 cup sugar
    3. 3/4 cup brown sugar
    4. 2 eggs
    5. 1 tsp vanilla extract
    6. 2 1/4 cups all-purpose flour
    7. 1 tsp baking soda
    8. 1/2 tsp salt
    9. 2 cups semisweet chocolate chips
- Instructions:
    1. Preheat oven to 350°F (175°C).
    2. Cream together butter, sugar, and brown sugar until fluffy.
    3. Add eggs and vanilla, mix well.
    4. In a separate bowl, combine flour, baking soda, and salt.
    5. Gradually add dry ingredients to wet ingredients, then stir in chocolate chips.
    6. Drop spoonfuls of dough onto a baking sheet and bake for 10-12 minutes.

Homemade Spaghetti Sauce

- Ingredients:

    1. 2 tbsp olive oil
    2. 1 onion, chopped
    3. 2 cloves garlic, minced
    4. 2 cans crushed tomatoes
    5. 1 tsp dried basil
    6. 1 tsp dried oregano
    7. 1/2 tsp sugar
    8. Salt and pepper to taste

- Instructions:

    1. Heat olive oil in a saucepan over medium heat.
    2. Add onion and garlic, sauté until softened.
    3. Stir in crushed tomatoes, basil, oregano, and sugar.
    4. Simmer for 20-30 minutes, stirring occasionally.
    5. Season with salt and pepper, and serve over spaghetti.

Fresh Lemonade from Scratch

- Ingredients:

    1. 1 cup fresh lemon juice (about 4 lemons)
    2. 1 cup sugar
    3. 5 cups cold water
    4. Ice

- Instructions:

    1. In a small saucepan, combine sugar and 1 cup water. Heat until sugar dissolves.
    2. In a pitcher, combine lemon juice, sugar syrup, and remaining 4 cups of cold water.
    3. Stir well, then serve over ice.

Homemade Vanilla Pudding

- Ingredients:

    1. 2 1/2 cups milk
    2. 1/2 cup sugar
    3. 2 tbsp cornstarch
    4. 1/4 tsp salt
    5. 3 large egg yolks
    6. 1 tsp vanilla extract
    7. 2 tbsp butter

- Instructions:

    1. In a saucepan, combine milk, sugar, cornstarch, and salt. Cook over medium heat, whisking constantly, until thickened.
    2. Whisk egg yolks in a separate bowl. Gradually add hot milk mixture to eggs, then return to saucepan.
    3. Cook for 2-3 minutes, then remove from heat and stir in vanilla and butter.
    4. Let cool, then chill for at least 2 hours before serving.

Crispy Chicken Tenders

- Ingredients:
    1. 1 lb chicken tenders
    2. 1 cup flour
    3. 2 eggs, beaten
    4. 2 cups breadcrumbs
    5. 1 tsp paprika
    6. 1 tsp garlic powder
    7. Salt and pepper to taste
    8. Oil for frying

- Instructions:
    1. Season chicken tenders with salt, pepper, paprika, and garlic powder.
    2. Dredge chicken in flour, dip in beaten eggs, then coat in breadcrumbs.
    3. Heat oil in a frying pan over medium heat and cook tenders for 4-5 minutes per side, until golden and crispy.
    4. Serve with your favorite dipping sauce.

Fresh Vegetable Soup

- Ingredients:

    1. 1 tbsp olive oil

    2. 1 onion, chopped

    3. 2 carrots, peeled and chopped

    4. 2 celery stalks, chopped

    5. 2 potatoes, peeled and cubed

    6. 1 zucchini, chopped

    7. 2 cups vegetable broth

    8. 1 can diced tomatoes

    9. 1 tsp dried thyme

    10. Salt and pepper to taste

- Instructions:

    1. Heat olive oil in a large pot over medium heat.

    2. Add onion, carrots, and celery, and sauté for 5-7 minutes.

    3. Add potatoes, zucchini, broth, tomatoes, and thyme.

    4. Bring to a boil, then simmer for 20-25 minutes until vegetables are tender.

    5. Season with salt and pepper and serve.

Warm Buttermilk Biscuits

- Ingredients:

    1. 2 cups all-purpose flour
    2. 2 tsp baking powder
    3. 1/2 tsp baking soda
    4. 1/2 tsp salt
    5. 1/4 cup cold butter, cubed
    6. 3/4 cup buttermilk

- Instructions:

    1. Preheat oven to 425°F (220°C).
    2. In a bowl, mix flour, baking powder, baking soda, and salt.
    3. Cut in butter until mixture resembles coarse crumbs.
    4. Add buttermilk and stir until just combined.
    5. Drop spoonfuls of dough onto a baking sheet and bake for 12-15 minutes.

Creamy Alfredo Sauce

- Ingredients:
    1. 1/2 cup butter
    2. 1 cup heavy cream
    3. 2 cups grated Parmesan cheese
    4. 2 cloves garlic, minced
    5. Salt and pepper to taste

- Instructions:
    1. Melt butter in a saucepan over medium heat.
    2. Add garlic and sauté for 1 minute.
    3. Pour in cream and bring to a simmer.
    4. Stir in Parmesan cheese until smooth.
    5. Season with salt and pepper, and toss with pasta.

Sourdough Bread

- Ingredients:
    1. 1 cup sourdough starter
    2. 1 cup water
    3. 3 cups all-purpose flour
    4. 1 1/2 tsp salt
- Instructions:
    1. In a large bowl, mix starter, water, flour, and salt.
    2. Knead for 10 minutes until smooth, then let rise for 2 hours.
    3. Shape dough into a loaf and place on a baking sheet.
    4. Let rise for 1 hour, then bake at 450°F (230°C) for 30-35 minutes.

Homemade Bagels

- Ingredients:

    1. 1 1/2 cups warm water
    2. 2 tbsp sugar
    3. 1 tbsp active dry yeast
    4. 4 cups all-purpose flour
    5. 1 1/2 tsp salt
    6. 1 tbsp honey
    7. 1 egg, beaten (for brushing)

- Instructions:

    1. Dissolve yeast and sugar in warm water and let sit for 5 minutes.
    2. Add flour and salt to the yeast mixture, knead until smooth.
    3. Let dough rise for 1 hour.
    4. Shape into bagels and boil for 1-2 minutes in water with honey.
    5. Brush with egg wash and bake at 425°F (220°C) for 20-25 minutes.

Classic Beef Stew

- Ingredients:

    1. 1 lb beef stew meat, cubed
    2. 1 onion, chopped
    3. 3 carrots, peeled and chopped
    4. 3 potatoes, peeled and cubed
    5. 2 cups beef broth
    6. 1 tsp dried rosemary
    7. Salt and pepper to taste

- Instructions:

    1. Brown beef in a large pot over medium heat.
    2. Add onions and sauté for 5 minutes.
    3. Add carrots, potatoes, broth, and rosemary.
    4. Bring to a boil, then simmer for 1-2 hours until beef is tender.
    5. Season with salt and pepper, and serve.

Apple Pie with Homemade Crust

- Ingredients:

    1. 2 1/2 cups all-purpose flour
    2. 1 tsp salt
    3. 1 cup cold butter, cubed
    4. 6-8 tbsp cold water
    5. 6 cups apples, peeled and sliced
    6. 1 cup sugar
    7. 1 tbsp lemon juice
    8. 1 tsp cinnamon
    9. 1/2 tsp nutmeg

- Instructions:

    1. Mix flour and salt, then cut in butter until crumbly.
    2. Add water and form dough, then chill for 30 minutes.
    3. Roll out dough, place in a pie dish, and add apple filling mixed with sugar, lemon, and spices.
    4. Top with a second crust, seal, and bake at 375°F (190°C) for 45-50 minutes.

Baked Ziti with Meatballs

- Ingredients:

    1. 1 lb ziti pasta
    2. 2 cups marinara sauce
    3. 1 cup ricotta cheese
    4. 1 1/2 cups shredded mozzarella cheese
    5. 1/2 cup grated Parmesan cheese
    6. 12 meatballs (cooked)

- Instructions:

    1. Cook ziti according to package instructions and drain.
    2. Mix cooked pasta, marinara sauce, ricotta, and half of mozzarella.
    3. Layer in a baking dish, top with meatballs, then sprinkle with remaining mozzarella and Parmesan.
    4. Bake at 350°F (175°C) for 20-25 minutes.

Creamy Tomato Soup

- Ingredients:

    1. 2 tbsp butter
    2. 1 onion, chopped
    3. 2 cloves garlic, minced
    4. 4 cups crushed tomatoes
    5. 2 cups vegetable broth
    6. 1 cup heavy cream
    7. Salt and pepper to taste

- Instructions:

    1. Melt butter in a pot, then sauté onion and garlic for 5 minutes.
    2. Add tomatoes and broth, bring to a boil.
    3. Simmer for 20 minutes, then blend until smooth.
    4. Stir in cream, season with salt and pepper, and serve.

Chicken Pot Pie

- Ingredients:
    1. 2 cups cooked chicken, cubed
    2. 1 cup frozen peas and carrots
    3. 1/2 cup butter
    4. 1/2 cup flour
    5. 2 cups chicken broth
    6. 1 cup milk
    7. 1 tsp salt
    8. 1/2 tsp pepper
    9. 2 pre-made pie crusts
- Instructions:
    1. Preheat oven to 375°F (190°C).
    2. Make filling: melt butter, whisk in flour, then add broth and milk.
    3. Stir in chicken and veggies, season with salt and pepper.
    4. Pour into a pie crust, cover with second crust, and bake for 40-45 minutes.

Fresh Raspberry Jam

- Ingredients:

    1. 4 cups fresh raspberries
    2. 3 cups sugar
    3. 1/4 cup lemon juice
    4. 1 packet pectin

- Instructions:

    1. Mash raspberries in a bowl.
    2. Combine with sugar and lemon juice in a pot.
    3. Boil for 5-10 minutes, then add pectin and boil for 1-2 minutes.
    4. Pour into sterilized jars and let cool.

Banana Bread from Scratch

- Ingredients:

    1. 2-3 ripe bananas, mashed
    2. 1/3 cup melted butter
    3. 1 tsp baking soda
    4. Pinch of salt
    5. 3/4 cup sugar
    6. 1 large egg, beaten
    7. 1 tsp vanilla extract
    8. 1 1/2 cups all-purpose flour

- Instructions:

    1. Preheat oven to 350°F (175°C).
    2. Mix mashed bananas and melted butter in a bowl.
    3. Stir in baking soda, salt, sugar, egg, and vanilla.
    4. Add flour and stir until combined.
    5. Pour into a greased loaf pan and bake for 60-65 minutes.

French Toast with Homemade Syrup

- Ingredients:

    1. 4 slices bread
    2. 2 eggs
    3. 1/2 cup milk
    4. 1 tsp vanilla extract
    5. 1/2 tsp ground cinnamon
    6. 1/2 cup maple syrup
    7. 1/4 cup water
    8. 1 tbsp butter

- Instructions:

    1. Whisk eggs, milk, vanilla, and cinnamon in a bowl.
    2. Dip bread slices into the mixture and cook on a buttered griddle over medium heat until golden.
    3. For syrup: mix maple syrup and water in a saucepan, heat until warm.
    4. Serve French toast with warm syrup.

Pulled Pork Sandwiches

- Ingredients:

    1. 3 lb pork shoulder
    2. 1 onion, chopped
    3. 2 cups BBQ sauce
    4. 1 tbsp brown sugar
    5. 1 tsp garlic powder
    6. 1/2 tsp smoked paprika
    7. Salt and pepper to taste
    8. Sandwich buns

- Instructions:

    1. Season pork shoulder with garlic powder, paprika, salt, and pepper.
    2. Place in a slow cooker with chopped onion, BBQ sauce, and brown sugar.
    3. Cook on low for 8 hours.
    4. Shred pork and serve on sandwich buns.

Homemade Granola Bars

- Ingredients:

    1. 2 cups rolled oats
    2. 1/2 cup honey
    3. 1/4 cup peanut butter
    4. 1/2 cup dried fruit (raisins, cranberries)
    5. 1/4 cup chopped nuts (almonds, walnuts)
    6. 1 tsp vanilla extract

- Instructions:

    1. Preheat oven to 350°F (175°C).
    2. Mix oats, honey, peanut butter, dried fruit, nuts, and vanilla in a bowl.
    3. Press mixture into a greased baking pan.
    4. Bake for 15-20 minutes, then cool before cutting into bars.

Focaccia Bread with Rosemary

- Ingredients:
    1. 3 cups all-purpose flour
    2. 1 packet active dry yeast
    3. 1 tsp sugar
    4. 1 cup warm water
    5. 1/4 cup olive oil
    6. 2 tsp salt
    7. 2 tbsp fresh rosemary, chopped

- Instructions:
    1. Dissolve sugar and yeast in warm water, let sit for 5 minutes.
    2. Add flour, salt, and 2 tbsp olive oil.
    3. Knead until smooth, then let rise for 1 hour.
    4. Roll dough into a rectangle, drizzle with remaining olive oil, sprinkle rosemary, and bake at 400°F (200°C) for 20-25 minutes.

Fresh Guacamole with Salsa

- Ingredients:

    1. 3 ripe avocados, mashed
    2. 1/2 red onion, finely chopped
    3. 1 tomato, chopped
    4. 1 lime, juiced
    5. 1 tbsp cilantro, chopped
    6. Salt and pepper to taste
    7. 1 cup salsa

- Instructions:

    1. Mix mashed avocado, onion, tomato, cilantro, and lime juice in a bowl.
    2. Season with salt and pepper.
    3. Serve with salsa on the side.

Homemade Chicken Noodle Soup

- Ingredients:

    1. 2 tbsp olive oil
    2. 1 onion, chopped
    3. 2 carrots, chopped
    4. 2 celery stalks, chopped
    5. 2 garlic cloves, minced
    6. 6 cups chicken broth
    7. 2 cups cooked chicken, shredded
    8. 2 cups egg noodles
    9. Salt and pepper to taste

- Instructions:

    1. Heat olive oil in a pot and sauté onion, carrots, celery, and garlic until soft.
    2. Add chicken broth, bring to a boil.
    3. Stir in chicken and noodles, and simmer for 10-15 minutes.
    4. Season with salt and pepper, and serve.

Homemade Ice Cream

- Ingredients:

    1. 2 cups heavy cream
    2. 1 cup whole milk
    3. 3/4 cup sugar
    4. 1 tbsp vanilla extract

- Instructions:

    1. Whisk together cream, milk, sugar, and vanilla until sugar dissolves.
    2. Pour into an ice cream maker and follow manufacturer's instructions.
    3. Freeze for 2-3 hours until firm, then serve.

Fresh Tortillas

- Ingredients:

    1. 2 cups all-purpose flour
    2. 1/2 tsp salt
    3. 2 tbsp vegetable oil
    4. 3/4 cup warm water

- Instructions:

    1. Mix flour, salt, and oil in a bowl.
    2. Gradually add water until dough forms.
    3. Knead dough for 5-7 minutes, then let rest for 30 minutes.
    4. Divide dough into 8 portions, roll into circles, and cook on a heated skillet for 1-2 minutes per side.

Sweet Potato Fries

- Ingredients:

    1. 2 large sweet potatoes, peeled and cut into fries

    2. 2 tbsp olive oil

    3. 1 tsp paprika

    4. Salt and pepper to taste

- Instructions:

    1. Preheat oven to 425°F (220°C).

    2. Toss sweet potato fries in olive oil, paprika, salt, and pepper.

    3. Spread on a baking sheet and bake for 25-30 minutes, flipping halfway through.

Classic Meatloaf

- Ingredients:

    1. 1 lb ground beef
    2. 1/2 onion, chopped
    3. 1/2 cup breadcrumbs
    4. 1 egg
    5. 1/4 cup milk
    6. 1/4 cup ketchup
    7. 1 tsp garlic powder
    8. Salt and pepper to taste

- Instructions:

    1. Preheat oven to 350°F (175°C).
    2. Mix beef, onion, breadcrumbs, egg, milk, ketchup, garlic powder, salt, and pepper in a bowl.
    3. Shape into a loaf and place on a baking sheet.
    4. Bake for 45-50 minutes, then serve.

Eggplant Parmesan

- Ingredients:

    1. 2 medium eggplants, sliced
    2. 1 cup breadcrumbs
    3. 1 cup grated Parmesan cheese
    4. 1 cup marinara sauce
    5. 2 cups shredded mozzarella cheese
    6. 2 eggs, beaten
    7. Salt and pepper to taste
    8. Olive oil for frying

- Instructions:

    1. Preheat oven to 375°F (190°C).
    2. Dip eggplant slices in beaten eggs, then coat with breadcrumbs and Parmesan.
    3. Fry in olive oil until golden, then place on a paper towel to drain.
    4. In a baking dish, layer fried eggplant, marinara sauce, and mozzarella cheese.
    5. Bake for 20 minutes, or until cheese is melted and bubbly.

Lemon Meringue Pie

- Ingredients:

    1. 1 pie crust (baked)
    2. 1 cup sugar
    3. 2 tbsp cornstarch
    4. 1 1/2 cups water
    5. 3 egg yolks, beaten
    6. 1 tbsp lemon zest
    7. 1/2 cup lemon juice
    8. 2 tbsp butter
    9. 3 egg whites
    10. 1/4 tsp cream of tartar
    11. 1/4 cup sugar

- Instructions:

    1. In a saucepan, combine sugar, cornstarch, and water.
    2. Stir in egg yolks, lemon zest, and lemon juice, then cook until thickened.
    3. Remove from heat and stir in butter.
    4. Pour filling into pie crust.
    5. Beat egg whites with cream of tartar, then add sugar and beat until stiff peaks form.

6. Spread meringue over filling and bake at 350°F (175°C) for 10-15 minutes.

Homemade Chocolate Cake

- Ingredients:

    1. 1 1/2 cups flour
    2. 1 cup sugar
    3. 1/2 cup cocoa powder
    4. 1 tsp baking soda
    5. 1/2 tsp baking powder
    6. 1/2 tsp salt
    7. 1 cup water
    8. 1/2 cup vegetable oil
    9. 2 large eggs
    10. 1 tsp vanilla extract

- Instructions:

    1. Preheat oven to 350°F (175°C) and grease two 8-inch cake pans.
    2. Mix dry ingredients in a bowl, then add wet ingredients and mix until smooth.
    3. Divide batter between the pans and bake for 30-35 minutes.
    4. Cool before frosting with your favorite frosting.

Perfect Scrambled Eggs

- Ingredients:
    1. 4 eggs
    2. 1/4 cup milk
    3. Salt and pepper to taste
    4. 1 tbsp butter
- Instructions:
    1. Whisk eggs with milk, salt, and pepper.
    2. Melt butter in a pan over medium heat.
    3. Pour in eggs and stir gently, cooking until just set.

Beef and Vegetable Stir Fry

- Ingredients:

    1. 1 lb beef (sirloin or flank steak), thinly sliced
    2. 2 cups mixed vegetables (bell peppers, carrots, broccoli)
    3. 2 tbsp soy sauce
    4. 1 tbsp oyster sauce
    5. 1 tbsp sesame oil
    6. 2 garlic cloves, minced
    7. 1 tsp ginger, minced

- Instructions:

    1. Heat sesame oil in a pan, cook garlic and ginger for 1 minute.
    2. Add beef and cook until browned.
    3. Add vegetables, soy sauce, and oyster sauce, stir-fry for 5-7 minutes.
    4. Serve hot with rice.

Rustic Italian Focaccia

- Ingredients:

    1. 3 cups all-purpose flour
    2. 1 packet active dry yeast
    3. 1 tbsp sugar
    4. 1 cup warm water
    5. 1/4 cup olive oil
    6. 2 tsp salt
    7. 1 tbsp rosemary, chopped

- Instructions:

    1. Dissolve sugar and yeast in warm water, let sit for 5 minutes.
    2. Mix in flour, salt, and olive oil.
    3. Knead dough for 5-7 minutes, let rise for 1 hour.
    4. Punch down dough, shape into a rectangle, drizzle with olive oil, and sprinkle rosemary.
    5. Bake at 400°F (200°C) for 20-25 minutes.

Fresh Peach Cobbler

- Ingredients:

    1. 4 cups fresh peaches, sliced
    2. 1/2 cup sugar
    3. 1 tbsp lemon juice
    4. 1 1/2 cups all-purpose flour
    5. 1/2 cup sugar
    6. 1/2 tsp baking powder
    7. 1/2 tsp cinnamon
    8. 1/4 tsp salt
    9. 1/2 cup milk
    10. 1/4 cup butter, melted

- Instructions:

    1. Preheat oven to 375°F (190°C).
    2. Toss peaches with sugar and lemon juice, then place in a baking dish.
    3. Mix flour, sugar, baking powder, cinnamon, and salt, then stir in milk and butter.
    4. Pour batter over peaches and bake for 35-40 minutes, until golden brown.

Homemade Donuts

- Ingredients:

    1. 2 cups all-purpose flour
    2. 2 tsp baking powder
    3. 1/2 tsp salt
    4. 1/2 cup sugar
    5. 2 eggs
    6. 1/2 cup milk
    7. 1 tsp vanilla extract
    8. 1/4 cup melted butter
    9. Vegetable oil for frying

- Instructions:

    1. Mix dry ingredients in a bowl, then add wet ingredients and stir until smooth.
    2. Heat oil in a deep pan to 375°F (190°C).
    3. Drop spoonfuls of batter into hot oil, frying until golden brown.
    4. Drain on paper towels and coat with powdered sugar or glaze.

Baked Chicken Parmesan

- Ingredients:

    1. 4 chicken breasts
    2. 1 cup breadcrumbs
    3. 1 cup grated Parmesan cheese
    4. 2 cups marinara sauce
    5. 2 cups shredded mozzarella cheese
    6. 1 egg, beaten
    7. Salt and pepper to taste

- Instructions:

    1. Preheat oven to 375°F (190°C).
    2. Dip chicken breasts in beaten egg, then coat with breadcrumbs and Parmesan.
    3. Place in a baking dish and bake for 25-30 minutes.
    4. Top with marinara sauce and mozzarella cheese, bake for an additional 10 minutes.

Creamy Mushroom Risotto

- Ingredients:

    1. 1 cup Arborio rice
    2. 1/2 cup white wine
    3. 1/2 cup grated Parmesan cheese
    4. 2 cups chicken broth
    5. 1/2 cup heavy cream
    6. 1/2 lb mushrooms, sliced
    7. 1 small onion, chopped
    8. 2 tbsp butter
    9. 1 tbsp olive oil
    10. Salt and pepper to taste

- Instructions:

    1. Heat olive oil and butter in a pan, sauté onions and mushrooms until soft.
    2. Stir in rice and cook for 2-3 minutes.
    3. Add wine and cook until absorbed.
    4. Gradually add chicken broth, stirring constantly until rice is cooked and creamy.
    5. Stir in cream and Parmesan cheese, season with salt and pepper.

Spicy Tuna Poke Bowl

- Ingredients:

    1. 1 lb sushi-grade tuna, cubed
    2. 1 tbsp soy sauce
    3. 1 tbsp sesame oil
    4. 1 tsp sriracha sauce
    5. 1 tsp rice vinegar
    6. 1/2 avocado, sliced
    7. 1/2 cucumber, sliced
    8. 1 cup cooked rice
    9. 1 tbsp sesame seeds
    10. Green onions for garnish

- Instructions:

    1. In a bowl, combine tuna with soy sauce, sesame oil, sriracha, and rice vinegar.
    2. Let marinate for 10 minutes.
    3. Serve tuna mixture on top of rice, garnished with avocado, cucumber, sesame seeds, and green onions.

Homemade Scones with Jam

- Ingredients:

    1. 2 cups all-purpose flour
    2. 1/4 cup sugar
    3. 2 tsp baking powder
    4. 1/2 tsp salt
    5. 1/2 cup cold butter, cubed
    6. 1/2 cup milk
    7. 1 egg
    8. Jam of choice for serving

- Instructions:

    1. Preheat oven to 375°F (190°C).
    2. Mix dry ingredients in a bowl, then cut in butter until mixture resembles coarse crumbs.
    3. Stir in milk and egg, forming a dough.
    4. Shape dough into a disk, cut into wedges, and place on a baking sheet.
    5. Bake for 15-20 minutes until golden. Serve with jam.

Hearty Breakfast Burritos

- Ingredients:

    1. 4 large flour tortillas
    2. 4 eggs, scrambled
    3. 1/2 lb cooked sausage or bacon
    4. 1 cup shredded cheese
    5. 1/2 cup salsa
    6. 1/4 cup sour cream

- Instructions:

    1. Scramble eggs in a pan.
    2. Cook sausage or bacon and chop into small pieces.
    3. Assemble burritos by placing eggs, meat, cheese, salsa, and sour cream in tortillas.
    4. Roll up and serve.

Classic Lasagna

- Ingredients:

    1. 12 lasagna noodles
    2. 1 lb ground beef
    3. 2 cups ricotta cheese
    4. 2 cups shredded mozzarella cheese
    5. 1/2 cup grated Parmesan cheese
    6. 1 jar marinara sauce
    7. 1 egg
    8. 2 tbsp fresh basil, chopped
    9. Salt and pepper to taste

- Instructions:

    1. Preheat oven to 375°F (190°C).
    2. Cook noodles according to package instructions.
    3. Brown ground beef, then mix with marinara sauce.
    4. Combine ricotta cheese, egg, basil, and Parmesan.
    5. Layer lasagna with noodles, meat sauce, ricotta mixture, and mozzarella, repeating layers.
    6. Bake for 30-35 minutes until bubbly.

Slow Cooker Chili

- Ingredients:

    1. 1 lb ground beef or turkey
    2. 1 onion, chopped
    3. 2 cans kidney beans, drained and rinsed
    4. 1 can diced tomatoes
    5. 1 can tomato paste
    6. 2 tbsp chili powder
    7. 1 tsp cumin
    8. Salt and pepper to taste

- Instructions:

    1. Brown the meat and onion in a pan.
    2. Transfer to a slow cooker with beans, tomatoes, tomato paste, and spices.
    3. Cook on low for 6-8 hours, stirring occasionally.

Creamy Shrimp Scampi

- Ingredients:

    1. 1 lb shrimp, peeled and deveined
    2. 8 oz spaghetti
    3. 4 garlic cloves, minced
    4. 1/2 cup white wine
    5. 1/2 cup heavy cream
    6. 1/4 cup butter
    7. 1/4 cup fresh parsley, chopped
    8. Salt and pepper to taste

- Instructions:

    1. Cook spaghetti according to package instructions.
    2. In a pan, melt butter and cook garlic until fragrant.
    3. Add shrimp and cook until pink.
    4. Stir in wine, heavy cream, and pasta.
    5. Toss with parsley, season with salt and pepper, and serve.

Blueberry Muffins

- Ingredients:

    1. 1 1/2 cups flour
    2. 1/2 cup sugar
    3. 1/2 tsp baking soda
    4. 1 tsp baking powder
    5. 1/4 tsp salt
    6. 1/2 cup buttermilk
    7. 1/2 cup melted butter
    8. 1 egg
    9. 1 cup blueberries

- Instructions:

    1. Preheat oven to 375°F (190°C) and grease a muffin tin.
    2. Mix dry ingredients in a bowl.
    3. In another bowl, whisk together wet ingredients.
    4. Combine both, fold in blueberries, and spoon into muffin tin.
    5. Bake for 18-20 minutes until golden.

Chocolate Fudge Brownies

- Ingredients:

    1. 1 cup butter, melted
    2. 1 1/2 cups sugar
    3. 3/4 cup cocoa powder
    4. 1/2 tsp baking powder
    5. 4 large eggs
    6. 1 tsp vanilla extract
    7. 1 cup flour

- Instructions:

    1. Preheat oven to 350°F (175°C).
    2. Mix melted butter, sugar, cocoa, and baking powder.
    3. Add eggs and vanilla, then stir in flour.
    4. Pour batter into a greased pan and bake for 25-30 minutes.
    5. Cool and cut into squares.

www.ingramcontent.com/pod-product-compliance
Lightning Source LLC
LaVergne TN
LVHW081326060526
838201LV00055B/2491